To Helen H.

MW00674715

1231 Love Street

Lula Holliday

Thank you
Evangelist Lula Holliday

Scripture references are taken from the Life Application Bible Copyright © 1991. Tinsdale House Publishing, and Zondervan Publishing

ISBN: 978-1-60383-041-6

Published by:
Holy Fire Publishing
Unit 116
1525-D Old Trolley Rd.
Summerville, SC 29485

www.ChristianPublish.com

Cover Design: Jay Cookingham

Printed in the United States of America and the United Kingdom

ACKNOWLEDGEMENT

To everyone who God has allowed to touch my life for my betterment , I thank you. To all who was not for my good, I thank you, too. For I know that in all things God works for the good of those who love Him, and who has been called according to His purpose (Romans 8:28). God had a purpose in mind for me in my hurts. He used you to help me get to this season and time in my life. I thank God for Bishop T.D. Jakes for he has helped me so much through his Woman Thou Art Loosed Conferences.

To my friend and mentor, Sister D. Miles, thank you for the advice you gave me through the years. To my friend and Sister D. Barclift: one who knows me better than anyone else, we have shared much through the years. Thank you for being my friend. To my pastor, Elder C.L. Sexton Jr, thank you for speaking life and truth to me at a time when I needed it the most. To Sister M. Lloyd, thank you for all the help you gave me in writing this book. May God ever bless you in your life's undertaking.

To God be the glory for all the great things He has done, and is doing in my life.

Table of Contents

CHAPTER 1
<u>HEY: THIS IS MY LIFE'S STORY</u>

When my father and my mother forsake me, then the Lord will take me up (Psalms 27:10).

I was born in Savannah, Georgia at 10 PM on Monday, January 25, 1944. I was a child born out of time; however, it was yet within God's timing. It was out of time because my mother and father were not married to each other (my father's wife was dead, and my mother was separated from her husband). So, within such a time, I was born; and under such circumstances, my problems began.

My father's name was Solomon Benjamin, but the last name on my birth certificate is Anderson. I never met the man whose last name I had been given. As a child, I did not know this, since I was raised by the Benjamin side of my family. However, the rest of the family did; and I was treated differently from the rest of the children on my father's side of the family.

I must admit that not all of my childhood was bad because I was raised by my two older sisters on my father's side. They were 12 and 13 years older than me. The younger one became my "mother" because she took care of me when I was small.

Shortly after I was born, my mother and father broke-up. My father's sister, Aunt Laura, kept me while my mother worked. When my mother decided that she was going to take me with her to Florida, Aunt Laura told my mother that she would have to pay her for every day that she had kept me while she had been working (at this time, I was about two years old). Later in my life, I was told that my mother brought me to Aunt Laura's house, and put me down in front of the house where my sister, Penny, was playing. When I began to walk toward my sister, my mother turned and walked away (out of my life for the next 12 years).

This is how I came to live at 1231 Love Street. I have some good and bad memories of that place. That block of Love Street was a "family block." There were about 40 kids on that block between Eagle and Ferrell Street. Our house was a four room attached house: ten houses all together. In those four rooms lived my Aunt Laura, my sisters (Mildred and Penny), and me. Aunt Laura was called "Big Sister" because she was the oldest sibling of my father's brothers and sisters, and I was called "Little Sister" because I was the youngest child of my father.

I had a good life, before Penney left home, when I was a child between the ages of 3-12 years old. This was because Penney who took care of me, and I thought of her like she was my mother. As a child, I had some of the best Christmas presents. I was the first one on my block with a talking black doll. I could wind her up and she would say her prayers: "Now I lay me down to sleep. I pray the Lord, my soul to keep. If I should die before I wake, I pray the Lord my soul to take. Please, Lord, teach me how to pray, and make me better everyday. Amen. I made money by charging other children a nickel to hear my doll speak (the kids really paid it).

I was the first one on my block to have a bicycle of my own that I didn't have to share with another sibling. I remember that Christmas so well because that was the year that I found out that there was no Santa Claus. I had been next door at my father's friend's house. When she sent me home, I came into the house and found Penney putting a red bicycle next to the Christmas tree. That marked the end of Santa Claus for me. Then, she explained to me, "Mommy is the Santa, and daddy is the Claus; put the two together, and you have Santa Claus." Boy did that hurt! I really believed that Santa Claus was a real person.

Four months later, my father pawned my bike to the grocery store owner, (Mr. Zipper: a White man) for twenty dollars. I never got my bike back. Many days I would pass his store and see my bike rusting away in his yard. After that, I didn't believe too much in Christmas, and I sure didn't believe in Santa Claus any longer.

CHAPTER 2
<u>Resilient Fighter and Warrior</u>

Blessed be the Lord my Strength, which teaches my hands to war, and my fingers to fight (Psalms 144:1).

My family was part White, Black, and Indian. My grandfather had a White father, and my great grandmother was an Indian. I was told that my great grandmother's hair was so long that she could sit on it. I was born with the shortest hair in the whole family, on both my mother's and father's side of the family. Penny's hair was long and pretty. Her hair was so long that you could roll it around your finger, and make it form a curl when you pulled your finger out of it. I always had short hair, but I grew to be the tallest of my sisters. I took after my grandfather who was 6 feet 2 inches tall. I am 5 feet 7 inches tall, which is tall for a lady, unless you are aspiring to be a model (smile).

Not only did I have the shortest hair in my family, was the tallest of my sisters, but also, I was fat. However, I thank God for small favors because He gave me the prettiest skin tone of all my sisters. I am also the only one who is save; although, two of my sisters were save. I am yet praying that, one day, they will give their hearts back to the Lord.

As a kid, I had a lot of fun growing up on my block, but I, also, had a lot of fights. We, kids, were a little mischievous, not because we wanted to be, but because of things that happened. In the middle of our block, we bought our cookies and candy from a "Mom and Pop" store. The store owner (a Black man), had a lot of plum trees in his back yard. We asked him if he would allow us to pick some of his plums and sell them to us for a dime a bag. His answer was, "no". He would rather let his chickens eat them than allow us to have some. He was known as "the mean man of the block." So, the older kids that lived next door to his house made a hole under his fence and covered it over. That night the older kids gave the younger kids (me and my friends) a few pennies to go into the store and keep the owner busy, while they were getting some plums from the trees in the back yard. His chickens were cackling, running around, and making a lot of noise, while we kept "the mean man" busy in the store. The next morning, he tried to figure out what had happened the night before. By then, the older kids had filled the hole back in and put the fence back in place. From that day on, he sold us plums for a nickel a bag.

The store owner was "the mean man" of the block, but there was, also, "a mean old lady" of the block. We kids played baseball in the street near her house because it was the best place to play ball. Because she had an empty lot next to her house, we could hit our ball and not get into trouble. But if we hit a ball into her back yard, she would not give it back to us, nor would she let us go into her yard to get it. So, one Halloween, we decided to get even with her. We had a firecracker: an H-Bomb. We lit it and put it in her mailbox. When it went off, we heard a noise that sounded like someone falling out of bed. It was the talk of the block the next day. Even though we knew what had happened, we said that we didn't know anything. The old adage says, "Hear no evil, see no evil, and speak no evil."

When I was a child, I had to do a lot of fighting because I didn't have any brothers and sisters at home to fight for me. I became the "girl bully" of the block, and Charles Reynolds was the "boy bully" of the block. If a girl could beat me, then she could rule the block; and if a boy could beat Charles Reynolds, then he could own the block.

The worst fight of my life was the day I was sitting on my front porch. The kids brought Queen (a girl who lived down the block) to my house to fight me. During the fight, Queen had gotten the best of me. I was down on one knee and was pushing myself up on the other knee, and was swinging upward with my left fist. Because I was looking down and swinging upward at that time, I didn't know that Aunt Laura had moved Queen out of the way. I caught Aunt Laura under her chin with a hard left punch. That was the end of that fight for that day. I had to remain on the porch for the rest of the day. I didn't get a beating because she knew I had to fight, or get beat up by someone everyday of the week.

That is how and why I became a fighter. I have been fighting all of my life. Even before I was born, I was fighting to stay alive. But that is

14

another part of my life's story that I will talk about in a later chapter of this book. God has put within each of us, before we were born, what we need to make it in this life. God said to Jeremiah (Jeremiah 1:5), "Before I formed you in the womb, I knew you. Before you were born, I set you apart. I appointed you as a prophet to the nation." God has given each of us what we need to become what he has proposed and planned for our lives; if only we would give Him our lives.

There were many days that I went hungry all day when I was a child until mommy came home from work. She would bring home the left-over from the White people's dinner for me to eat. Sometime mommy would cook for Mr. Zipper when Mrs. Missie was out of town. Mom and I ate many meals because of Mr. Zipper. He would also let me watch his television because we didn't have one. I would watch the Mickey Mouse show, Buffalo Bob, The Little Rascals, and some other children's shows.

CHAPTER 3

GOD'S HAND ON MY LIFE

If it had not been the Lord on my side when men rose up against me, then I would have been swallowed up quick when their wrath was kindled against me (Psalms 124:2-3).

My life changed forever after my sister, Penney, left home. Daddy nearly stopped taking care of me. I didn't have decent clothes to wear, sometimes Aunt Laura and I didn't have food to eat, and every month, there was a "For Rent" sign on the door of our house. My daddy always had a good job. He worked for Meddon Brother's Meat Packing Plant. He transported live stock from town to town in Georgia, and to different states in the south. So, he had money!

Penney was the only one who could get money out of daddy. She could get whatever she wanted, whenever she wanted it, and how much she wanted. Years later, while I was reading her birth certificate, I learned the reason why she had such a special place in his heart. Daddy was the one who caught her when she came out of her mother's womb. Two weeks later, her mother died. That was the reason he loved Penney with all his heart. Even when he was dying, he only called for her to come and see him.

The most hurtful thing I remember about my father was that he just didn't believe that I was his child. I believed that because of two things he did and said to me. One day (when I was between 11 or 12 years old), Aunt Laura told me to go to daddy and ask him for some money to buy food. When I told him what she had said, he pulled down my pants and panties, and looked at my private area. Then he pulled them back up, and told me not to tell Aunt Laura about what he had done.

About a year later, mommy sent me again to get money from him. This time he was in the bed. He said to me, "If you want me to give you some money for food, get in bed with me." I said, "No!! Daddy," and backed out of the door, and went home. When Aunt Laura asked me about the money, I told her that he didn't have any. I never told her what he had said to me. From that day forward, I never wanted to be alone with my father. I just couldn't understand a father saying such things to his own child. Shortly after that incident, I ran away from home.

After that incident with my father, mommy (Aunt Laura) was the only one I had left to take care of me. She worked in "Cracker Town," cooking and cleaning in White people's houses. At one point, she sold moon-shine to take care of me. Daddy was not doing much at that time, but working; however, he still didn't give mommy any money to take care of me, as he could have, or should have.

I never knew mommy to go to church, but she made sure that I went every Sunday. I went to church with my Aunt Annie, and my two cousins (who lived with Aunt Annie and her husband and my grandmother, Old Miss). The name of our church was St. Marks Baptist Church, which was located on Louisville Road. I was on the junior usher board and a Sunday school member. I, always, liked to read the Bible and talk about Christ. Even before I got save, God had a purpose for my life; just as He has for you, too. At one time, I remember that my sister, Penny, was going to go to the doctor because she was real sick. I laid my hands on her and began to pray. Then, she said that she didn't feel anymore pain. Also, I used to tell people things that came true.

As I got older, I began to call Aunt Laura, "mommy", because she did whatever she could for me. When the lady that she worked for would give her old clothes, she would cut them down, so that they would fit me. Mr. Zipper would give her flour sacks with flowers on them. When mommy would get two of the same kind, she would make a skirt and blouse. She would bleach the flour sacks that were white, and make slips for me.

The only thing that I hated about mommy was when she was with Aunt Annie, or when she got upset with me. She would say that, "You're never amount to anything. You're going to be just like your mommy (my real mother), no good." It's so funny how people can blame the child for what the mother and father did or did not do.

The first time I ran away from home, I was trying to get away from my father. My real mother was living in Savannah again. I ran away to stay with her. But she would not let me stay with her. She tried to send me back home to daddy. She didn't know what daddy had said to me. Instead of going home, I went to stay with my oldest sister on my mother's side of the family. Her name was Mildred, too. Penney was living in the downtown area. She caught me one night, and called the police. I didn't know that my father had a missing person bulletin out on me. The police took me back home to my daddy. I was only fourteen years old, then. Who could I have told about my father; or who would have believed me? I thank God that he never said or did anything sexually abusive to me again. I was so afraid of my father that I ran away from home again. This time I went to live with a school friend and her family. That was the beginning of a great change in my life.

On New Year's Eve Night 1959, I had my first encounter with my Lord Jesus Christ. I remembered it so well. I was in my room by myself praying as we always did on New Year's Eve. We were taught to pray the old year out and the New Year in, so this is what we always did. You could find anyone from the south in church, ten minutes before midnight, praying until midnight.

I began to pray. I said to the Lord, "Lord I'm so tired of living the way I'm living. If you save me, I will do whatever you want me to do." All of a sudden, I felt like I was lost in a cloud of love. I could not tell you how wonderful it felt. There was so much love in that room that I began to look around to see if there was someone in there with me. There was such a sweetness in the room. I got up off my knees because I heard someone saying, "Happy New Year." I never told anyone about what happened to me that night. About a year later, I went to stay with my real mother in Hitchvillage on the east side of town. I lived with her until I met Billy Holliday, and until we got married.

CHAPTER 4
GOD'S LOVE IN MY LIFE

For God is love (1 John 4:8b).

I was about 16 ½ years old when I went to stay with my real mother (Susie Mae Kennell). I had four sisters: Mildred, Peggy, Lonnie Mae, and Laverne, and one brother on my mother's side of the family. My mother had moved into a housing project. It was a nice place with three bedrooms, kitchen, living room, and a nice size bathroom. I got a job across from the old Sears store off of Henry Street. I worked as a dishwasher for Mr. Pano.

My friend, Effie Lee, was seeing a boy named Spooky at the time, and Billy was Spooky's best friend. I was seventeen when I started seeing Billy. I had known Billy most of my life because he lived a block and a half from my house. But it seemed like we lived worlds apart. His family was the haves, and we were the have-nots. The Hollidays lived in their own home. His mother owned her own beauty shop. Their father worked at the Sugar Refinery. He drove a new car. Because his sister went to Savannah State

College, she had her own car to drive to school. Billy's other sisters and brother went to Catholic School.

Billy was good-looking, dressed nice, and smelled good. He was all any girl would want in a boyfriend. On the other hand, he had a problem. When he started drinking, he would get drunk so fast that his body just could not handle the liquor. He came to my house, and asked my mother permission to see me. She gave her approval.

When I lived in West Savannah, I had a lot of lies told on me by boys because I didn't have a lot of nice clothes to wear. Another reason they told lies on me was because I hung out with some bad girls during those times, which gave me a bad reputation. That did not mean I was a loose girl; I just didn't have any other friends who wanted to be with me. Billy found out for himself that I was not like that. Because he knew me better than any other man ever knew me, I loved him.

I will admit that we got married too young, but John was his child, and he knew it. About seven months after we got married, Billy left Savannah and came to New York, and got a job at Creedmore Hospital. Three months later, John and I came to New York to be with him. I spent my first night in New York at his grandmother's house on Stone Ave. in Brooklyn.

One Friday night, three weeks after I came to New York, everyone was going to service at Billy's grandmother's church. This was a small store front sanctified church on Utica Ave. near Fulton Street. Since I was studying to be a Catholic, I didn't want to go with them. However, I didn't want to be left alone at the house because everyone else was going to this sanctified church. So, I went with them, and sat three rows from the back of the church.

Boy, were they having a time in that church. People were singing, dancing, and making a lot of noise. I just sat there, looking around. All of a sudden, a young girl jumped up, and started dancing. I said in my heart, "Whatever she has that makes her act like that, I want it, too." I turned around and gave John to Billy. When I turned back around, I started crying like a baby, and I didn't know why I was crying like that. Billy's, Aunt Babe, told me to go to the altar where there were two chairs in the front of the

24

church. As soon as my hands touched the chair, I hit the floor, and there I met the Lord, again. I was down on that floor for about forty-five minutes. Every time I would try to get up, down I went again. I didn't claim salvation that night, but God finished the job on me some months later.

I remembered a dream I had had before I left Savannah. I had a dream that my sister, Penny, had come home from New York. She gave me a white A-line dress, but it was too big for me. I went to the hotel to give it back to her. When I got there, someone had just mopped the floor. It was the whitest floor I had ever seen. I went to the desk, and asked for my sister. The man had a big book in his hand, and told me that her name was not there. He said there was a place for a new name. Then I woke up.

I told Billy's mother about the dream. She said that it had something to do with someone having a clean life. One day, at Billy's grandmother's house, I began to tell them about the dream. His cousin went into her grandmother's closet, and came out with the same white dress I had seen in my dream. I was so shocked that I didn't know what to say. It was so strange how God had let me dream something, and then let me see it in real life.

About three months later, we moved to a house on Legion Street, between Sutter and Blake Ave. We lived there with Billy's Aunt Minnie. One Friday night, while I was on my way to a R. Shambach Revival Meeting, I passed a store front church on Sutter Ave. For some reason, I went in there, and joined the church the next week. I was going to that church, when my son, John, got sick. He was about seven months old when he began to have seizures. His eyes would roll back in his head, and he would shake all over. We took him to a doctor to find out what was wrong with him. The doctor gave me some medicine to give John, and said, "At his age, if he continues to have seizures, and if he lives, he will be a vegetable the rest of his life."

I refused to give John the medicine. I told Billy and his sister, "I am not going to give John this medicine. I am going to take him to church, and let the saints pray for him, for only God can heal him." They thought that I was crazy. On a Tuesday night, two days before Thanksgiving in 1962, I took my son to church for prayer. My pastor took John in his arms. The saints made a circle around him. He anointed John, and began to pray for him. From that day, 41 years ago, John never had another seizure. As a matter of fact, he finished high school, did a year of college, is an elder at our church, has five children, and is a correctional officer. I praise God for his healing power. If God can't do it, then it can't be done. Genesis 18:13-14 says, "Then the Lord said to Abraham, Why did Sarah laugh and say, Will I really have a child, now that I am old? Is anything too hard for the Lord?" Of course not, if you can believe, God can and will do it, if it is His will. God only wants what is best for us.

CHAPTER 5
<u>I FEAR NO EVIL</u>

Yea though I walk through the valley of the shadow of death, I fear no evil: for God is with me, His rod and His staff comfort me (Psalms 23: 4).

During the early years of my marriage, I was having babies real fast. I had one full term child, after John, who was breech (butt first) at birth. He died at birth. My next child, Craig, was healthy. There were no problems with his birth. However, the next pregnancy wasn't so blessed. But for the goodness of God, I am alive today.

I don't know how to really explain it. Some may call it an out-of-body experience. I had gone to the hospital because I was spotting real badly, and it was not time for that to be happening. The doctor checked me out, and gave me some medicine to take. He said that I was to take it easy for a few days. The next day I was alone in the house with the kids because Billy had gone to work to get his check. While in the bathroom, I got a pain in my lower back that was so bad that I could not stand up. When I was able to get up, I had to hold on to the wall, and slide myself along until I got to the bed. I got my blessed oil, and began to pray. Soon after that, Billy got home, and saw that I was sick. He called an ambulance. When they got there, they tried to put me in a wheelchair. I was told that when I tried to stand up, my eyes rolled back in my head, and I went down. When I woke up, I was on a table in the examination room. The doctor was asking me questions, but I was going in and out of consciousness. He didn't seem to know what was wrong with me. He finally called the head GYN doctor. That doctor told me that I was pregnant in the tubes, and that I had to have an operation if I wanted to live. He said that he would give me a few hours to think about it because he needed my permission to do the surgery. I remember that I was lying on a table in the hallway when, suddenly, I was in the present of someone who was all love. I was consumed in His presence. He said to me, "Have your operation. I am going to give you your life back." This is why I believe it was an out-of-body experience. I was caught up in His presence. When I came back to reality, I saw the doctor coming down the hall. He said to me, "Mrs. Holliday, are you ready to have your operation now. I said, "Yes." I looked at the clock. It was 7 AM.

The next thing I remembered was waking up in the recovery room. Because I was so cold, I asked for more covers. When someone gave them to me, I was out again. The next time I woke up, I was being wheeled to my room. I had been in the operating and recovery room all day. It was night when they placed me in my bed. When the doctor came to check on me, he said, "Mrs. Holliday, do you know that you were more dead than you were alive. You had three pints of blood pushing upward in your stomach. The baby in your tube was rotten, and the poison was traveling throughout your system." I was cut from one side of my stomach to the other. I was given blood because I had lost so much. On top of all that, I was told that I would not be able to have anymore children.

I had two boys, and I really wanted a little girl. But I believed, if God said no, then it was no. But Guess What!!! A short time later, I got pregnant again. I said, "Lord, let it be a girl. Please, let it be a girl." That child was Tonia Denice Holliday. I was 22 ½ years old. I never got pregnant again. Not only did God give me my life back, He gave me my heart's desire: my little girl.

God is a good God. If we would love Him, and serve Him, He will do what Psalms 37:4 says, "Delight yourself in the Lord, and He will give you the desires of your heart. Proverbs 3:5-6 says, "Trust in the Lord with all your heart; and lean not on your own understanding. In all your ways acknowledge Him, and He will make your paths straight." God is a life-giving God.

CHAPTER 6
<u>VENGEANCE IS MINE</u>

Dearly, beloved, avenge not yourselves, but rather give place unto wrath; for it is written, Vengeance is mine; I will repay, says the Lord (Romans 12:19).

Have you ever had something happen to you unexpectedly (like suddenly; out of the blue, so to speak). Well, my husband had a way of doing things "out of the blue." One night while I was praying in my bedroom, Billy came in drunk, with a bottle of Old English 800 in his hand. He said to me, "Have a drink. This will help you pray better. I got up off of my knees because I just couldn't believe what he had just done. He looked at me, and turned and left the apartment.

Around four o'clock the following morning, there was a knock on my front door. When I opened the door, there was a policeman there. He asked me if I was Mrs. Holliday. I told him, yes. Then he asked if I had a husband named Billy Holliday. Again, I said, yes. He told me I had to be down at the Brooklyn Court House early in the morning Because Billy had been arrested, and his case would be heard, then.

After I got the children off to school, I went to the court house. While I was sitting in the court room waiting for Billy's case to be called, the Holy Spirit said to me, "Look behind you." As I turned around and looked, a big (approximately three hundred pound) policeman came in the room. The Holy Spirit spoke to me again and said, "That is the policeman who arrested your husband." When they called his case, he came in the court room with his pants and shirt all ripped up. He had bruises on his arms and back. The judge asked, "Who brought this man in my court looking like this."

The same policeman that the Holy Spirit had shown me, got up and went before the judge. He said, "I did, Your Honor. I arrested him in the Ralph Ave. train station, pissing on the steps. He resisted arrest, and I had to fight with him. Now, I am out on sick leave. The judge told the policeman to never bring another person into his court room looking like that.

Because it was Billy's first offense, and he had a job, the judge just fined him, and let him go.

Billy told me later on that the policeman hurt his hand when he tried to hit Billy. Billy said that he ducked, and the policeman hit the wall. The Holy Spirit said to me, "You could not say or do anything when he offered you that drink while you were praying to me. But, I could."

Sometimes we want to react when someone says something bad to us, or does us wrong. But God said that He would fight our battles, if we would just keep still. The battle is not ours to fight, it's the Lord's. Billy received a good beating that night from that policeman. God's hands were behind it all. The battle was not mine, it was the Lord's! You shall not need to fight in this battle: set yourself, stand still, and see the salvation of the Lord with you (2 Chronicles 20:17).

CHAPTER 7
GOD'S PROVISIONS

My God shall supply all my need according to His riches in glory by Christ Jesus (Philippians 4:19).

When the city condemned the building we were living in on Pacific Street, my children and I stayed with my sister-in-law: Shirley, my brother's wife. They had a room big enough to put a bed in. I put the boy's bunk bed in it. John and Craig slept on the top bunk, and Tonia and I slept on the bottom bunk. John was about 10 years old then, Craig about 8 years old, and Tonia about 6 years old. We slept like this for about five months, while I looked for an apartment. John asked me, "Mom, what's going to happen to us. I told him that God would take care of us. During this time, Billy had gone home to Savannah to get a job, but, instead, he ended up in jail.

Before I moved from my sister-in-law, I got a letter from the Housing Authority about an apartment. At the appointment, they gave me three choices to choose from. I chose the

Kingsborough Houses as my first choice because I had lived down the block from it for 6 years. Soon I found a place that I could afford. It had a bathtub in the kitchen with a steel slab over it. The toilet was in a small closet. I thanked God for it. It had two bedrooms. John and Craig slept in their own beds, and Tonia and I slept together. I moved there because the Housing Authority had said that the waiting list was two years long, and that it would take that amount of time before I would be called for an apartment. When God's timing comes, what God has for you, no one can keep it from you.

About a month after I moved into the new place, I got a letter from Kingsborough Housing to come for an interview. I was asked a lot of personal questions at the interview (about my family, and our living conditions). I told him the truth about everything. Two weeks later (just before Labor Day), I was told to come and get my keys. After Labor Day, when I went for my keys, I was told that I couldn't have the apartment because it only had one bedroom, and that I needed two bedrooms because I had boys.

I was praying all the time. Then, I began to tell God what I wanted: not just an apartment, but a two bedroom apartment. I prayed, "I needed it now! Lord, Now!!" In less than a week, I was told that they had an apartment for me, but that it had to be painted, and I could come and see it. On my way into the building, I met a woman that I knew from the Laundromat. God had given me a place where I had known a lot of the people for years. God placed me on the first floor of 320 Kingsborough 3rd Walk, Apt. 1C.

God will make a way for you, if you will just trust Him, and remain faithful to Him in your hour of need. Hold on to Him, no matter how hard or dark the times may seem. God will make a way out of no way. He will speak doors in your life. Where there is no door, God will speak, and an open door will appear.

CHAPTER 8
<u>I AM NOT FORSAKEN</u>

*What shall I say to these things? If
God is for me, who can be against
me (Romans 8:31?*

While Billy was in jail, God blessed the children
and me to move into Kingsborough Housing.
Because, it was so much better than any place
that we had been living before, it was like
moving on up to the East side; we finally had
our piece of the pie. I worked hard as a presser
so that I could fix up the apartment before Billy
got home. He was gone for about 3 years.

During that time, we (the kids and I) had a lot of
good times together. Not that we had much, but
we had each other. I always tried to make sure
that my kids had a good Christmas. Every year,
around the first of October, I would put their
toys on lay-a-way at Mays Department Store;
then around the last of November, I would get
them out of lay-a-way and take the toys to
Mother Murray's house. I did this all by myself
until John got old enough to help me out.

We would sing Christmas carols every Christmas Eve before we went to bed. Early Christmas morning, before day break, I would go get the kid's toys, and put them in the living room. One Christmas, I bought the kids a Hockey table. One day, I came home from work, and the house was full of children from the neighborhood. Craig, always business minded, was charging the kids to play a game of hockey on his table. I bought Billy a console with an eight track tape player, radio, and a recorder. I also, bought him some new clothes so that he would look nice when he came home.

My first plane trip was when I went home to pick up Billy, when he was getting out of jail. I stayed strapped in my seat the whole ride. I thank God; we came back to New York by bus. God blessed him with a job, two weeks after he got back. Things were going good for about 6-7 months; then things began to happen.

Billy became friends with the guy he worked with on the truck. Billy introduced him to our next door neighbor, she introduced Billy to her best friend, and they started going out together. Before I got saved, Billy and I would go out dancing a lot: he loved to party and drink. After

I got save, I was told that I could not party like I did before. So Billy found other women to party with. I was left home, alone, hurting and crying.

We had week night church services on Tuesday and Friday nights. I tried staying home on Friday nights because he said that I was going to church too much. I would stay home, but when it became too late for me to go to church, he would get up, start an argument, get dressed, and go out. He was a good looking man, so it was not hard for him to have lady-friends. Sometimes he would go out our door, go to the front door of the building, turn around, come back inside and knock on the door next to ours, and go in.

I cried and prayed many days because I didn't want to "act out." I knew what was going on: the phone calls that would go dead when I answered them. One night I followed the two ladies around the corner to the bar. When they got there, Billy was outside waiting for them. When he saw me, he said, "What are you doing here? Go home!" Not long after that, he lost his job; and when he lost his job, he lost his girl friends.

Being unemployed, he was home all the time. I was the only one working. I made enough money to take care of the bills, and the needs of the house because I would work overtime each Saturday. After Billy lost his job, he became mean to me and the children. He was drunk most of the time because he used his unemployment check to get drunk. He became abusive toward the boys. John was about 14 and Craig was about13, at this time. I had to talk to my boys a lot during those times to keep them from jumping their father, and beating him up when he got drunk.

One day, I got on the train at Jamaica Ave. and 121st Street, and by the time I got home I was as sick as a dog. Day after day, that would happen to me. I would me fine until I got on the train to go home. Because stress could have and would have killed me, I began to pray about this sickness and the reason for it. The Lord told me to tell Billy that he had made a vow to Him, and that if he didn't keep that vow, he would never be able to rise up again. When I got home, Billy was on the sofa drunk as usual. I sat down on a chair, and told him what the Lord had said to tell him. He was very quiet. I got up and went into the bedroom to change clothes.

Billy came in the doorway, and said to me, "Sis, you are right. I did make God a vow. I want you to pray for me." Then he turned and walked away. He never told me what the vow was. Ecclesiastes 5:4-6 says, "When you make a vow to God, do not delay in fulfilling it. He has no pleasure in fools; fulfill your vow. It is better not to vow than to make a vow and not fulfill it. Do not let your mouth lead you into sin."

If there ever was a man I wished that I could save, it would have been Billy because in my heart, he was the love of my life. No matter what, I loved him. Some people grow up, some never do. If only he had grown up, we would have been together until he died. For he was the first man that was willing to show me that he really cared about me.

CHAPTER 9
<u>ANGER, HURT, AND</u>
<u>THEN RAGE</u>

Every man is tempted when he is drawn away of his own lust, and enticed. When lust is conceived, it brings forth sin, and when sin is finished, it brings forth death (James 1:14-15). Therefore, be angry, but sin not; neither give place to the devil (Ephesians 4:26:27).

Have you ever tried to fight a battle that was not yours to fight? I did, and I lost it. But, for the grace of God, I am here today. There were two days involved: October 31st, and November 1st. On October 31st: Halloween, The church was having a party for the children, although it was not called a Halloween party. It was just an activity that kept the kids off the streets because so many bad things happened on that night.

I had promised some of the kids on the block that they could go to church with me and my kids that night. When I got home from work that night, some of the kids were at my house waiting for me. Billy came in and wanted to know what was going on, and I told him. He got a chair from the living room, and put it against the door. He started cursing, and said that nobody was going anywhere. I sent the kids home, and told them that I was sorry that I would not be able to take them to the party at the church. After the kids left, Billy told John and Craig to go to bed, and I had to go to bed, too.

The next morning, I was tired, and angry about the night before. I had to go to work, but Billy was still asleep. When I came home from work that day, no one was home. I decided to take a nap. Before I went to bed, I saw a tree stump that one of the boys had brought in the house. I looked at it, and said to myself, "If Billy comes in this house, this day, and start a fight; I am going to take that club, and hit him as hard as I can." I went to sleep. About two hours later, Billy came in drunk, and started in on me. How could he want me to go to bed with him, when he smelled so bad, and was calling me everything except a child of God? Oh how the devil don't care. I got so angry that I got the club off the floor and swung. I missed him, but broke the light on the side of the wall. He hit me in my eye, and I still have trouble with that eye today.

In all the years I had been save, I don't remember fighting Billy; I had only tried to keep him from hurting me. I never had wanted to fight him. I had always prayed, and asked God what I should do. That day, I had been pushed to the point where Lula came back with all her fighting ways. I was some how able to get away from him, and get out of the house; but since I was not dressed to go out into the street, I had to go back into the house. I went to my neighbor's house and called the police. Before they got there, Billy opened the door for me. He had a bat in his hand, and backed me out of the building into the court yard with the bat in his hand.

Two young men that we knew came over to him, and began talking to him. He dropped the bat, and I picked it up. The moment the bat touched my hand, I was a different person. All I heard was, "Hit him for every time he made you cry; hit him, hit him, hit him!!" Then it changed from "hit him" to "kill him, kill him, kill him!!" I swung that bat so hard that I could hear the wind in my ear from the force of me swinging that bat. I don't know what he saw in my eyes, but he started running, and fell. I was about to hit him in the head, when one of the young men caught me by both of my shoulders. I heard him say, "Mrs. Holliday, don't do it; it's not worth it!" I came to myself, dropped the bat, and cried, "Oh God, you have to do something, now! I have wanted him to leave; I have wanted him to die, but never have I wanted to kill him. God you have to do something for me, now!'

About that time, the housing police arrived. They told Billy to get what he needed out of the house: his clothes, and leave. He was told not to come back in the house, unless he came and got one of them to go with him. They told me to go to the office, and get a form and give it to Billy so that his name could be taken off the lease; then the apartment would become mine.

I did what the policemen had said. Billy signed the papers, and the apartment became mine. Billy and I never stayed together again. I thanked God that the children were not at home that day. John was with his Godmother; Tonia was with Sis. Barclift; and Craig was working at the church. When Craig got home and found out what had happened, the first thing he said was that I should have killed the nigger. Where peace and love had been, now, there was hate, anger, and pain. Parents, whatever you do, don't let your children see you argue and fight with your spouse because you don't know what affect it will have on your children.

That was one day I fought a fight that was not mine to fight. Some years later, I asked God, "Why did you let me go that far." He said to me, "Because you had already said what you were going to do." If you are a child of God, never tell God, or speak in your mind, what you are going to do. Proverbs 3:5-6 says, Trust in the Lord with all your heart, and lean not on your own understanding; in all your ways, acknowledge Him, and He will make your paths straight. I didn't pray and ask God about what to do. I said that I was going to hit him, if he messed with me. Anger, hurt, and hate had taken over in my heart. I wanted to hurt him for every time he had hurt me. At that point in time, I had forgotten that God had said, "Vengeance is mine, I shall repay."

I thanked God, many times, for having those young men there that day. Because they were there, I didn't do what the Devil had wanted me to do: that was to kill Billy. If I had killed Billy, my children would not have had me because I would have gone to jail. Even though I had gone too far, God's grace (His unmerited favor) was there. He allowed me to hear that young man's voice that said, "Don't do it, Mrs. Holliday; it's not worth it." I was walking and thinking in my own way. I didn't cast my cares on Him like He told me to do, yet His mercy and grace was there to cover me.

If you get caught up in something, and go too far, don't give up. Get up, and remember that God yet loves you. He will forgive you, if you just ask Him.

CHAPTER 10
<u>IN THE HANDS OF A</u>
<u>MIGHTY GOD</u>

The arrogance of man will be brought low and the pride of men humbled: The Lord alone will be exalted in that day (Isaiah 2:17 LAB).

In the previous chapter, I told about what happened the day (but for the grace of God) that I almost killed Billy (because he was trying to kill me). He left the house, but he didn't leave us alone. He would come by the house and try to get in when the children got out of school. One day, as he was standing on the steps, he had Craig knock on the door. When John opened the door for Craig, Billy pushed his way into the house. He took off his clothes, got in my bed, and waited for me to come home from work.

John waited until he was sound asleep; left the house; met me at the Ralph Ave. train station; and told me what his father had done. We went straight to the Kingsborough Housing Police. A police officer escorted us back to the house. Billy was still asleep in my bed. Boy was he ever surprised to be awakened by the police officer and to see him standing over him! The policeman told him to get up, to put his clothes on, and to get out of the house. He never came into the house gain, but he would meet me (on the street, or at the train station) when I was coming home from work. He would curse me and call me all kinds of names, but he never hit me again. The day before he backed me out of the house with a bat, he gave me a knife and said, "Let's see who can kill who, first." I dropped the knife on the table, and backed out of the door, and into the court yard of the complex, and the rest is history. Listen, my sisters, if you find yourself in a situation like I was in, do whatever you have to do to **"Get Out Of It!"** In the 1970's, we didn't have much help because there were no shelters for battered women. Now, there are many shelters where you can receive the help you need to get out of a life threatening situation. Listen ladies, your life, health, state of mind, and salvation are worth far more than staying in those kinds of circumstances for any reason.

God doesn't want you to be stressed out. Cast all your anxieties on Him because He cares for you (1 Peter 5:7 LAB). Whether your husband is save or not, the Bible says, "In this same way, husbands ought to love their wives as their own bodies. He who loves his wife loves himself. After all, no one ever hated his own body, but he feeds and cares for it, just as Christ does the church (Ephesians 5:28-29 LAB). No one in his/her right mind will misuse his/her own body. If you two are supposed to be one; how can he mistreat you if he really loves you?

However God has given you a remedy: No temptation (problem or trouble) has seized you except what is common to man. And God is faithful; He will not let you be tempted beyond what you can bear. But when you are tempted, He will also provide a way out so that you can stand up under it
(1 Corinthians 10:13 LAB). My sisters, don't go as far as I did. Let God give you a way to get out of it. For you see, I told God what I was going to do if Billy came into the house and started in on me ("I'm going to hit him as hard as I can with this tree stump"). **WARNING!!** You just may go too far: he may kill you, or you may kill him; and then what?

Remember to: "Trust in the Lord with all your heart and lean not on your own understanding; in all your ways acknowledge Him, and He will make your paths straight. Do not be wise in your own eyes; fear the Lord and shun evil. This will bring health to your body and nourishment to your bones (Proverbs 3:5-8 LAB)." If you heed the warning, then you will not grow old suffering with an eye and ear problem (like I have) that I received that day fighting with Billy. Let God be your fire escape. Live to see God exalted in your life the day when you become free, happy, and healthy in mind, body, and spirit.

CHAPTER 11
<u>MY SUFFICIENCY</u>

My grace is sufficient for you: for my strength is made perfect in your weakness (2 Corinthians 12:9). My God shall supply all my needs according to his riches in glory by Christ Jesus (Philippians 4:19).

After Billy left for Savannah to stay, God, the church, and my children was all I had left. My children were always close to me, but we became even closer. John was about 14, Craig 12, and Tonia 10 years old when their father left home for the last time. Because John was the oldest, he became the man of the house. He was one of the original latch-key kids. He wore the key on a chain around his neck, and he was responsible for letting Craig and Tonia in the house after school.

Because John was always my quiet child, he suffered more abuse from his father than Craig and Tonia. Billy would call him names: like stupid and dumb. He would say to him,

"What's wrong with you, don't you know anything?" I thought it was because he blamed John for our getting married at such a young age, but we really didn't have to get married, then. It was a choice we both had made.

But Billy really loved Craig, though. Craig was his boy because he was more athletic than John. Craig was always outside, playing some kind of sports. Not that John was disinterested in sports; he liked sports also, but he preferred to watch television a lot.

Parents should never let their children know that they love one child more than they love the other child, nor should they put one child before the other. Each child had their own personality. Years later, when John was 40 years old, as he was standing at the foot of his father's death bed, he said, "This man has caused me more pain than anyone else in my life." He had never voiced anything like that to us before. He had held that hurt in his heart all those years. Parents should realize that their children may never tell you how they really feel about what you say to them or what you do or don't do for them, but they have feelings, too.

One time before Billy left, I took my bank book with $250.00 in it, and got on the A train. I didn't know where I was going; I just knew that I had to get away. I could not take the pressure any longer. I just wanted to get away from it all: the children, Billy, the drinking, and the fighting. I was just so tired.

I don't know how long I was on that train, maybe two hours; but God began to talk to me. The Holy Spirit said to me, "Go back home, your children are going to make you the woman I want you to be, and you are going to make them the children I want them to be." I went back home, and never told Billy what I had left home to do.

My children and I came through some hard times together. There were days when we didn't have enough to eat, but we always had something to eat. I had a seasonal job. I worked as a presser from February to November, and sometimes we started back to work in March. During that time, I was on unemployment. My unemployment was not as much as my regular pay check, but with God's help, we made it.

When the boys were old enough, they got their working papers. John and Craig worked, during the summer, for the Housing Authority, cleaning up the grounds around the project. With the money they made, they were able to buy their school clothes. When Tonia was old enough, she had a baby sitting job, and she worked at the Fulton Street Mc Donald Restaurant. When the Housing Authority stopped giving out summer jobs, Bro. Eddie Bland helped John get a messenger job. John had been playing basketball at Boys and Girls High School, but because I needed his help, he stopped playing basketball, and got that messenger job to help me. Craig got a job working in a grocery store to help out.

John was always my right-hand man around the house because he stayed around the house more than Craig. Craig was always out playing some place.

All three of my children finished high school: John from Boys and Girls High School, Craig from George Westinghouse High School, and Tonia from W.H. Maxwell Vocational High School. Each one of them did at least a year in college; however, Craig was the only one who finished. He received his BA from the College at Old Westbury. I never had a problem with my children drinking or smoking. Craig got drunk one time and vomited all over the bedroom. Tonia gave him a good talking to, and I don't know of him getting drunk ever again. When I could no longer beat Craig, God gave me to talk with him. Years later, he told me that my talking to him was worse than my beating him.

When Billy left for the last time, I went back to school. I went to Brooklyn Technical College and got my GED. Because of the conditions at home when I was a child, I dropped out of school in the 8th grade. I also, did a year in college. I dropped out of school again because I was working each day and sometimes on Saturday, and because I was doing piece work. Because I got paid so much on the dozen, I had to work real hard just to make $50-$60 a day; plus I had to come home and cook, and help as much as I could with the kid's homework. Math was always the most difficult subject for me.

CHAPTER 12
GOD'S WISDOM ABOVE ALL

If any lack wisdom, he should ask God, who gives generously to all without finding fault; and it will be given to him (James 1:5). Get wisdom, get understanding; do not forget my words or swerve from them. Do not forsake wisdom, and she will protect you; love her, and she will watch over you. Wisdom is supreme; thereforeget wisdom. Though it cost all you have, get understanding (Proverbs 4:5-7).

Sometimes, when you are a mother trying to raise boys alone, it seems like you are fighting an uphill battle because they think of Mom as a pushover; and when they reach a certain age, they want to act like they're a man. I began to see a change in each of my boys when they got about 13 or 14 years old. They got a little harder to handle; and yet, I tried not to be so hard on them.

In some Holiness churches, children were not allowed to play ball or do a lot of things that other kids did. I didn't want to break the spirit of my boys, so I prayed and asked God for wisdom and the ability to understand them. I allowed my children to play ball, go to ball games, and to go swimming. In other words, I allowed my children to be children. I tried to let my teenagers enjoy their teen years while growing up in a Christian home.

Some of us, who are 50 years and older and grew up in a Christian home with saved parents, have forgotten how we felt when we were teenagers. The reason many of us are trying to recapture our youth is because we couldn't wait to get grown so that we could leave home and have some of the fun that we were not allowed to have as children when we were children. But now is the time to "Grow Up and Learn How to Grow Old Gracefully!!" Now is the time to teach today's youth how to enjoy their youth, and to prepare them for adulthood. Children need discipline. They need to know what they can and can not do in the home without a man's presence.

Even though, John acted as the man of the house, he still had to obey me, and not the other way around. Mothers, stand up and be the mother in your home. Have rules that must be obeyed. Too many parents are letting their children rule them. I am reminded of a time when I had to do something that I did not want to do to my boys. I had given them permission to go to a school party, and had given them a time to be home. When that time came (I had waited another half hour) and went and they were still not back home, I got a chair, put it behind the front door and sat in it. When they returned home and John put the key in the door, I told them "don't come in because I allowed you to go to the party, but I also gave you a time to be home and you disobeyed me, so you can sleep in the hallway tonight." I sat in front of the door all night. In the morning, when I opened the door, they were sitting on the steps half-asleep. I never had a problem like that again. Mothers, love your children, do all you can for them, but have some rules in your house that you will not allow them to break at anytime or for any reason without them having to pay the consequences for their disobedience.

God has given parents a job to do: that job is to train our children. Train a child I the way he/she should go and when he/she is old he/she will not turn from it (Proverbs 22:6). If you lack the wisdom (of what to do, how to do, and when to do), then ask God for it. Study the word of God, pray, and learn to understand your child. For what you teach them as children will last them a lifetime. Don't do what you don't want them to do (drink, smoke, or use bad language). Don't have a new uncle staying with you every other month (need I say more). Model the behavior you want them to have. Live holy like God requires you to live.

CHAPTER 13
BY PRECEPTS AND EXAMPLES

Bring them up in the nurture and admonition of the Lord (Ephesians 6:4b): That from a child, they may know the holy scriptures, which are able to make them wise unto salvation through faith which is in Christ Jesus (2 Timothy 3:15).

I raised my children the best that I could. I took them to church. It could be said that they were a part of the "in-born generation" because all of their young life, they were in church. I taught them to respect their elders: to never talk back to an older person, whether they were right or wrong. That's the way I was raised. I taught them the importance of getting an education so that they could get out of the ghetto, and come back and get me out. I taught my children self-esteem: that they were somebody; that they could be anything or anybody they wanted to be; and that their success was up to them. I taught them that the world didn't owe them a living, but that it was up to them to make it for themselves.

Sometimes, John and Craig fought each other when they were teenagers. There were three of those fights that they had that I particularly remember. One of them occurred early one morning before they left for school. I can't remember what it was about, but I had to call the housing police. Before they got there, I had broken-up the fight. The police asked if everything was alright. I looked at both of them, and answered, "Yes." Another fight they had was while I was at work. Tonia called me and said that Bubbie (Craig) and Warren (John), (the names she called her brothers), were fighting, and that Bubbie had cut Warren on the leg. I left my job, came home, and ("Thanks be to God") found that he only had a flesh wound. The last fight that I remember them having was the one in which they were fighting in the bedroom, and I jumped between them. One moment, I was standing in the bedroom, and the next moment, I was standing in the hallway. John had picked me up and put me outside the bedroom door.

My boys were bigger and taller than I was, at this time. Craig was about 6 ft. 2 inches tall. I told him, "If I have to stand on a chair, hit you on the top of your head, tell you to fall down, you better lay there until I tell you to get up because I am the mother in this house, and you are going to obey me." I realized that I could no longer beat my boys the day I hit Craig on the shoulder, and he brushed it off as if a fly had landed on it. I stopped and looked at him as if I was seeing him for the first time. Don't get me wrong. I gave out some real good beatings in my day: the ironing cord was my best weapon.

John and Tonia did not get many beatings, but Craig was a different story. He would always try me. I always gave my children the chance to do right, but after the third wrong, they got a beating. I would wait until early in the morning, go in their room while they were sleeping, pull back the covers, and go to work. Craig could do more praying when he was getting a beating: "Oh, God, Oh, Lord, and so on." One night he slept under his bunk bed all night to keep from getting a beating. Sometimes, when I was beating him and he would start praying, I would stop beating him to go into the next room to laugh.

Tonia didn't get many beatings. She would tell on everyone else. She would meet me every day after I would return home from work, and give me the daily news report on John and Craig. One day she even called me on my job to tell me that no one was home and she couldn't get the top off of the peanut butter jar (to her, it was a big thing). I think, I told her to make a jelly sandwich. John was always the one around to help when I needed it, although, Craig would help if I could catch him.

Even though Craig would be the one to try my patience, he had a way of making me feel loved. He would come up to me, (no matter what I was doing), put his arms around me, just hold me for a few minutes, let me go, and walk away without saying anything. When I was a child, I don't remember anyone hugging me, or telling me that they loved me. The first time Craig did it, I tried to push him away, but the Spirit told me to let him do it because he had a reason for doing it that I did not know about. And even today, he still does the same thing, but now he kisses me and says, "I love you, Mom."

Sometimes, we look for love in all the wrong places. When God wants to show or give us real love, we don't know how to receive it. God used the hands and arms of my son, Craig, to hug me with. He used John to show me that he was a present help in the time of need because the money John made on his job helped me with a lot of Craig and Tonia's school clothes. Finally, he used Tonia to keep me abreast of what was happening at home when I was at work. Just like he told me on the A train, I am still seeing his word come to pass in my life. It was not always easy. Many days I prayed and asked God to help me and teach me how to be a mother to my children, and he did just that.

I never said or did anything in front of my children that would cause them to think less of me as a Christian and mother. This is the reason why the next chapter was so hard for me to write because my children knew nothing about my fall. Nevertheless, the Lord told me to write it because it would let someone else know that if they fall into sexual sins, God is willing to forgive them and will forgive them; if they will repent; ask for forgiveness; and be willing to let Him rule in their lives again.

CHAPTER 14
<u>OH, THE TONGUE</u>

The tongue is a little member, and boasts great things (James 3:5); therefore, give no place to the devil (Ephesians 4:27).

By now I guess you are wondering if she did anything wrong. "Yes, I did many times." I talked too much and got myself in trouble with God. Early in my Christian walk, God gave me the gift of prophecy. The first time God used me to bring a warning to my church, I had only been saved for about five years, and I really didn't know how to use the gift. I got hurt badly by what happened after I revealed the warning to the church. Therefore, I spoke out against my pastor. Then the Holy Spirit said to me, "Who are you to judge another man's servant? To his own master he stands or falls. And he will stand because the Lord is able to make him stand." I found the scripture in Romans 14:4.

Yes, the prophecy did come to pass, but I was wrong for saying and feeling the way I did. Years later, I was faced with the same problem. God taught me mercy and compassion through what happened to me. I will advise everyone to never say what you will or will not do. For in our nature lies the ability to do anything sinful. If we don't walk in the Spirit of God, and don't know the Word of God, we will obey the lust of the flesh, and our desires will get the best of us and cause us to sin.

About ten years after the incident with my church, I became involved with the same thing that was going on in my church. At that time I was no longer a member of that church. After my husband had left New York, gone back to Savannah to live, and we had gotten a divorced, I met a young man four years younger than my ex-husband. He was just what I wanted. He was about 6 feet 2 inches tall, nicely built, good looking, and he had a job. But, he was not save!! He began to come to church with me, he enjoyed the services, and I thought that he would get save. I was lonely and tired of being by myself. When my emotions kicked in, all of my teachings and learning went out the window. Warning: "Never let your emotions rule you because if you do, they will cause you to sin." This man came to church with me until he got what he wanted. After I fell, things began to change.

I no longer could talk to him about the Lord. He would make fun of my beliefs. Another warning, "You can not say one thing and do another thing with the world. If you do, they will talk about you and the God you say you believe in." In Matthews 7:6, Jesus said, "Do not give dogs what is sacred: do not throw your pearls to pigs. If you do, they may trample them under their feet, and in turn tear you to pieces. The person never loved me. He wanted me, and when he got what he wanted, it was all over except the hurt and the shame. I cried because of how I felt, and what I had done. One day, while I was crying to God and repenting for what I had done, I told God that He had to help me because I could not do this by myself. He was still trying to talk to me, but the devil never gave up on me once he had me down. He wanted to see how far he could carry me down.

This young man moved out of the neighborhood, then began to call me. One night he called and said that he was coming over just to talk to me about something. I waited up until 11 o'clock that night, looking and listening for that knock on the door that never came. I was in the church, I was save, but at that time, my relationship with Jesus was not strong because of my "emotions. After I had cried to God about it again, the Lord began to talk to me. He said, "Do you remember when you cried to me that you could not handle the relationship any longer? You asked me to fix it. Well, this is how I fixed it. So, what do you want now?"

God was saying to me, "Do you want it to continue, or do you want to live for me?" I made the choice to live for the Lord and let the relationship go. However, I can't say that it was easy, for it was not easy! That relationship taught me not to say what I will or will not do. It also, taught me to have compassion and mercy on those who fall. This is the reason the Bible says for us to walk in the Spirit so that we would not obey the lust of the flesh. About four years later, I got a call from that same person wanting to see me again. I told him, "Leave me alone, and make a life for yourself." After a few more words, I hung up the phone. Seven months later, I heard that he had gotten married.

The devil will never give up on you. He will send James, John, or whatever their names maybe to try you again and again. But, I am a witness that with God's help, you can make it.

70

You can come out of it and live to see the glory of God moving in your life.

CHAPTER 15
LIVID

Wrath is cruel, and anger is outrageous (Proverbs 27:4).

My mother came back into my life when I was about twelve years old. Before that time, I had lived with my Aunt Laura, whom I called mommy. When I met my mother, she was living on the east side of town with my two sisters and one brother. She had come back to Savannah from Florida to live. I knew my brother because he had come to stay with us one summer, but I didn't know my mother or my sisters.

When I got older and ran away from home to get away from my father, I tried to stay with my mother, but she would not let me stay with her. Sometimes, I would spend a week or a weekend with her, but she would always send me back to my father. At one point, when I was staying with my older sister (on my mother's side); Penney found me and called the cops. They took me back home to my father.

I always tried to be respectful to my mother; I never said anything disrespectful to her. I guess I had just gone through so much hurt, pain, and disappointment that I had mentally hid it all in my mind, and I did not want to think or talk about them. There were some things that I had totally forgotten about until many years later in my life. Some of these things resurfaced when I went home to visit my mother in the early part of the 1990's.

Because my mother had Diabetes, one of her legs had been amputated. She was living with my youngest sister and her children on the east side near Savannah State College. She was in her bed, and began reminiscing about old times when I was a child. I don't remember what she said, but I said to her, "No, Mom, it was not like that." Then she said, "Yes, it was because I know!!!"

Somewhere deep inside of me, a dam broke. It was like a flood gate had opened up, and I began to remember things. When I came to myself, I was knocking on the walls, banging on the furniture, and talking loud. I was so angry that I could taste the rage in my mouth. I told her, "You don't know because you were not there! You don't know what those people put me through! You don't know what they said about you! You don't know what they have said or done to me over the years!" My mother just sat in that bed and looked at me with her eyes as big as they could be. I said to her, "You kept sending me back to them. Each time I tried to come and stay with you, you would send me back there. You just don't know what I went through!!!"

I told my sister that I was sorry for acting the way I had. She said that it was ok because she had been talking to mom about some of the same things I had said. For the rest of the day and most of the next day, I didn't say anything to my mom, and she didn't say anything to me. When my sister got home from work, she spoke to me, and asked me what was wrong with us, and why we were not talking to each other. I had spent most of the day in prayer. I was able to tell my mother that I was sorry: not for what I said because it was the truth, but for the way that I had said it. After that day, my relationship with my mother changed. I could talk with her more openly like a mother and daughter who were close to each other could talk.

My mother came to visit me in New York twice before she died. New York was a bit much for her because there were too many people, too much noise, and it was too fast. She was save and sanctified before she died, and was a church mother at her local church. However, by this time, she had lost both of her legs to Diabetes.

One day my mother said to me that she had done everything within her power to keep me from coming into the world, but that she was glad that I had made it because she was proud of me, and the way I had turned out. In an earlier chapter of this book, I told you that God put into you, before you are born what you need to make it in life. God had put a fighting spirit in me before I was born because I had to fight to get here, and once I got here, I had to fight to stay here. Through all that I have suffered: my mother not wanting me, my father not loving me, and two failed marriages, God yet said to me, "Have not I commanded you to fight. Fight your way to me!" God even allowed my mother and me to make peace with each other, and allowed her to make peace with Him before she died. Now, I am looking forward to seeing her in Heaven when I get there in the rapture, or in death.

With the help of God, I was able to make peace in my heart with my father because God gave me comfort. I believe my father believed in his heart that I was not his daughter. I have peace in my heart with that, and that is the way I am going to leave it. Some times we want to be delivered from all of our problems. God never told me that He was going to deliver me. He always told me to walk through it. I have learned many things by just walking through my problems with God.

CHAPTER 16
<u>FORGIVE TO BE FORGIVEN</u>

Forgive us our debts, as we also have forgiven our debtors (Matthews 6:12).

My two sisters, on my father's side of the family, came to New York a few years before me. Mildred the oldest, lived in the Bronx, and Penny in Brooklyn. They both are now dead. The oldest was the first to die. Before this, I had not seen them for a number of years because, when they had come out to Queens to help with our aunt when she was sick, something was found to be missing, and the family had a falling out about it. After that, they stopped calling me for about six years.

The first call I got, after the family's misunderstanding, was to tell me that Mildred was dead and buried. I was not told that she was sick until after she was dead. At that time, I didn't know how or where Penny was. Penny was the one that had taken care of me when I was a child. All I was told was that Mildred was dead. I did not try to find out more because of the hurt I had experienced at the family break-up over our aunt. Things were said at that time that was not so nice. I was the last one to know anything about the family, anyway. I was never in the loop; I was always "the last man out." So, I guess that I just didn't want to be a part of the family. Besides, I had my own family to worry about, and I really didn't need them, anyway.

I was busy being save and working in the church. I didn't have time to remember them, nor did I want to. I decided to "let sleeping dogs lie;" to forget about the old hurts (that way I didn't have to remember), so that I could forgive to be forgiven. About six years ago, I got a call that Penny was sick and her husband, Johnnie had died the year before. This signified how "out of the loop" I was with my father's side of the family. Even though they always had my phone number, I was always the last to know anything about the family.

During the phone call, I was told where Penny was living in Brooklyn, so I went to see her. When I got there, she was not home. I talked to some of the people in her building. One lady in her building told me something about Penny's housekeeper that I didn't like, but she said that I would have to find out about it for myself. When I was about to leave, I saw two women coming toward the house. One of them was very small. As I looked at the small lady, I knew she was Penny. I was surprised and shocked at how small she was. Penny had always been very heavy (about 250 lbs.), but at that time, she looked like she was only about 120 lbs.

At first, she didn't recognize me. She stood there and looked at me, and asked me who I was. Then, she said "Little Sister, and hugged me." That was the first time I had seen her in six or seven years. She couldn't remember much because her mind would come and go. She couldn't even tell me much about what had happened to her because she just couldn't remember. This was about a month before she died, but during that time, God gave me a chance to forgive her. However, it was not so much to forgive her as it was for me to forget and be forgiven for the things that I had said that I was not going to do because of the way the family had treated me.

I took her by my church, her old neighborhood, and the house that she used to live in, but she was not able to remember them. I told her about my children and grandchildren. Later, I got a call from her housekeeper (who turned out to be a nice person after all) that Penny was in the hospital. I went to see her that night. I didn't know that it would be the last time I would see her alive because she died sometime during that night from AIDS. God gave me a chance to love and forgive my sister again.

Unforgiveness is going to cause many to miss out with God because it can be the hardest thing for us to say "I'm sorry, or I forgive you." When we pray the Lord's Prayer, we pray "Forgive us our debts as we forgive our debtors." In other words, we are praying "Father, only forgive me, if I have forgiven those who have wronged me."

CHAPTER 17
GRACE TO LIVE

But He said to me, "My grace is sufficient for you: for my power is made perfect in weakness. That is why, for Christ sake, I delight in weakness, in insults, in hardships, in persecutions, and in difficulties: For when I am weak, then I am strong (2 Corinthians 12: 9, 10).

There are only four of us living on my mother's side of the family: me, my oldest sister, and my two younger sisters. My brother died after being shot in the head while being robbed and my sister (the one after me) died in her sleep. Now our family is trying to come together in love and forgiveness for each other.

For the last two years, I have been going home to spend time with them. I really want to know my family and to love and understand them better in our weakness, hardships, and difficulties. We don't always like the things we sometimes do, but that doesn't mean that we don't love one another. Last year we had a mini-family reunion in Augusta, Georgia at my niece's house. All of us that could have been there was there. We had a crab bake and lots of fun. We sat around (in my niece's back yard) on the pool deck while the younger ones swan in the pool. We took pictures and had a good time.

I'm so happy about what God is doing in my family. It took a long time, but we are finally coming together as a family. I'm praying that God will use me in whatever way he chooses to make us a true family. I'm still praying for my two sisters who fell from grace: for God still loves them. I hope and pray that they and all of my family members would get save, and come to know God: Jesus Christ as their personal savior. Mom would be so happy if she could see all of us up in heaven: because one day, we are going to have a great big family reunion in heaven. God's grace is sufficient for you, me, and all of our needs. For the grace of God has given me the strength to be strong enough to forgive and forget: that was one of my greatest weaknesses.

When I said Unforgiveness was one of my greatest weaknesses, it was because I had so many people to forgive: my mother, father, and my family on both sides. Within the last 15 years, God has brought me to a place in Him that I have forgiven everyone in my heart. I have no more Unforgiveness in my heart that I know about. Some people can't tell me that they are sorry because they are dead; and some really don't know that they have hurt me (like my younger sister). This happened at my mother's grave site. We were fussing about a flower that I wanted to bring home with me, but she said that I could not have it. She didn't know how hurt I was over that one flower (which is dead by now), but I just wanted that flower. I forgave her because I loved her and she loved me. Love covers a lot of things. Above all, love each other deeply because love covers over a multitude of sins (1 Peter 4:8). Therefore, for Christ's sake, I delight in weakness, in insults, in hardships, in persecution, and in difficulties. For, when I am weak, then I am strong.

As I have said before, when you pray, "Forgive us our debts, as we also have forgiven our debtors," remember that you are saying, "Father, only forgive me if I have forgiven the one who has did me wrong." Additionally, remember that if we can't forgive, we have forgotten how much God has forgiven us because our sins were the reason Christ went to the cross.

CHAPTER 18
<u>UNDERSTANDING ME</u>

Wisdom is supreme; therefore get wisdom. Though it cost all you have, get understanding (Proverbs 4:7 LAB).

Years ago, when I was a child, I would hurt myself, just to get attention. I remember cutting myself on my foot with a piece of glass just to get that attention. The scar is still visible today. Everyone wants to be loved, but until I learned to love myself for whom and what God had made me, I really didn't know what love was.

I was always a giver: I gave of myself and my time; I gave to make and keep friends; and I gave to my children because they needed me. I did not worry much about myself because I stopped needing the attention and started giving the attention to others. The more attention I gave to others, the better I felt about myself because that is what love is all about (giving, doing, and sharing with others).

When I got save, God began a work within me, and on me. He gave me three gifts of the Spirit: 1. Prophecy, 2. Teaching, and 3. Healing. God has used me in the first two gifts (Prophecy and Teaching) many times, but the last one (Healing), He has used in me only once since I have been save. I had wondered about that gift for a long time. Back, in the 1990s, Sis. Barclift talked me into going to Bishop TD Jakes' Woman Thou Art Loosed Convention. The first day, I was judging everybody in the place (their dress and their actions). However, before I left there that day, I found myself, down on my knees between the seats, calling on God and crying out to Him. God began a work in me that day. A new ministry to help hurting women (women who have been through or is going through the same/similar things like as I went through) was birthed (or awakened) in me. God let me know that this is my Healing Ministry. This Healing Ministry was to be a healing of the mind (the emotions and the intellect) rather than, so much, a healing of the body.

Some of my worse hurts have been mental pain. Whereas, physical pain lasts for a while, mental pain can last a lifetime. Many women are hurting and need help. Some time, no doubt, most of the time, we go to church and no one addresses these issues. We hear messages about married life, or what young people are doing or not doing. At our conventions, in between the fellowshipping, we hear some preaching, teaching, praying, and singing. Our emotions are stirred, but the issues remain unaddressed.

There were many days that I went to church and did not want to go in because I felt like no one understood what I was going through. At church, the atmosphere was "God Bless You, good to see you, and pray for me." Pray for you! Pray for what? You come in smiling, you leave smiling, and you seem to be the happiest person on earth, so what do you need prayer for? Prayer is needed for that different story that's going on behind the closed doors. Some of our homes had come apart: our husbands had left us for someone else, or we were never married in the first place and just stayed together. Whatever the issues were, we were hurting and living with it day after day, week, month, and year after year. The mental pain caused us to become baggage handlers, carrying old baggage from one relationship to the next because we were never healed.

When we came into the church, we believed that things would be different, but found that the pain was still there. We just learned to wear a mask to cover the signs of the anguish and pain. Don't get me wrong, however. God was there for me, although, it would have been much easier if someone would have said, "Sister, I know what you are going through. I've been there. I am here for you, if you need me."

I thank God for my friend, Barclift, who convinced me to go to that TD Jakes' Woman Thou Art Loosed Convention. I have gone almost every year since that first one I attended. I have learned so much about myself (how to love myself and others; how to forgive for the mistakes I've made and the sins I've committed; and how to forgive those who have wronged or hurt me).

Like I said in an earlier chapter, within the last 15 years, God has brought me a long way. Now I know who I am, and why He brought me the way He did. One day I asked the Lord, "Why was it, when I was going through (with Billy and my children; not having a nice place to live; and not having enough food to eat), that the family did not help me by sending a few dollars a month to help me out." God told me that He did not will it to be so. Because, if people were to help me all the time, I would never have been able to have the relationship He has allowed me to build and have with Him. God did not want me to lean on people and what they could do for me, but to lean on Him and Him alone.

Now I understand myself (my purpose, and my reason for being who I am). And, I love myself now! I now understand that my body is the temple of the Living God, and that I am to treat it as such. Psalms 139:14-16 (LAB): I praise you because I am fearfully and wonderfully made; your works are wonderful, and I know that full well. My frame was not hidden from you when I was made in the secret place. When I was woven together in the depths of the earth, your eyes saw my unformed body. All the days ordained for me were written in your book before one of them came to be. God knew me, and He knows me. He knows everything about me, just as he knows everything about you (your hopes, dreams, heartaches, and hurts. He knows us, and yet He loves us.

I thank God for my new Pastor because he addresses the women issues in his preaching and teaching. Also, I thank God for our National

Mother of the Church of God in Christ, Mother Willie Mae Rivers, who takes the time to talk to the younger women (40 years old and younger) at our International Women's Convention. Sister let's talk because you are talking to another sister. Girl, I've been there! I have done that, and I'm here to tell you that God can and will bring you out of that (whatever your particular **that** might be). However, you must want to come out of it, and to be free from the pain of the mental hurt you have received (no matter where or through whom it came). Learn to understand yourself; and when you do, you will come to know that God loves you enough to give you hope in a hopeless situation and peace in the midst of your storms. You will understand yourself as you grow in the knowledge and understanding of God.

CHAPTER 19
PEACEABLE LIVING

Blessed are the peacemakers, for they will be called the sons of God (Matthews 5:9 LAB).

In the previous chapter, I stated that there were some people who couldn't tell me that they were sorry for the way they treated me because they were dead. One of them was my only brother. My brother was the second child born to my mother by her husband (Mr. Anderson). He was the only boy among five girls. So you know that he was spoiled rotten. We all called him Bro (that was his nickname).

When he came to New York from Savannah, Bro and his wife lived with me, Billy, and our kids. He also had our sister's daughter with him whom he was raising as his own. Bro soon found a place down the block from us. As time went on, I saw less and less of my brother. He began to have a lot of money, nice clothes, and a new car. I didn't know how or where he got the money. I only knew he was a butcher by trade, and that he didn't make that kind of money as a butcher. I didn't find out what he was doing until a few years later.

One day, he told me that he was going home for a visit soon, and that he had some money (about a thousand dollars) that he wanted me to keep for him for the trip. I told him that I would put it in my bank account for him. He said he would come to my job at lunch time and we would go to the bank together. The day that he came to the job, it was raining and we had a hurried order that had to go out. So, I gave him my bank book and told him to go take care of the transaction at the bank , and to bring my bank book back by the house. The next day, he gave me back my bank book. About a month later, I drew the money out and gave it to him. He went home like he had said that he was going to do.

Three months later when I went to the bank to cash my check, I was told by the teller that I had to speak to the bank president. He told me that some checks were placed in my account that was stolen from the Federal Government, and that they would have to take the money out of my account to cover the stolen checks. I told her that I knew nothing about any checks. Then, she asked me if anyone had access to my bank book. It hit me like a "ton of bricks", my brother!!

I was so mad with him I couldn't work the rest of the day. I could only think that I trusted him enough to let him hold my bank book (something I had never did before) and he did this to me. My brother!! I was closer to him than any of my sisters. When I saw him the next day, I was as hot as "a smoking 45." He said that I was too trusting; and believed everything nice about people. He said that I shouldn't trust anyone. He gave me my money back; however, the FBI came to my job to talk to me because they were looking for him. My first visit to the World Trade Center was to go to the FBI's office for a handwriting test. My handwriting didn't match any of the signatures on the stolen checks so they didn't put me in jail. Bro did a few years in jail because it turned out to be a big thing that he was involved in (hundreds of thousands of dollars of stolen checks).

A very important lesson I learned from my brother was to never trust anyone completely (no matter how much you love and respect them. I maybe wrong, but that is the way I feel. I loved my brother, but I never trusted him again.

I forgave him, but it was hard for me to forgive myself. How could I have been so dumb? Sometimes, love will make you act without thinking. My brother never said that he was sorry for what he had did, and our relationship was never the same. Even though I forgave him, when some things in life get broken, they are never the same again.

Therefore, if you want to have peace with God, yourself, and your peers, there are some things you must do: 1. To have peace with God – Trust in the Lord with all your heart and lean not on your own understanding; in all your ways acknowledge Him and He will make your paths straight (Proverbs 3:5-6 LAB); 2. To have peace with yourself – Do not be anxious about anything, but in everything, by prayer and petition, with thanksgiving, present your requests to God (Philippians 4:6 LAB), and Cast all your anxieties on Him (Jesus) because He cares for you (1 Peter 5:7 LAB); and 3. To have peace with your peers and people – Never speak in anger, you may say the wrong thing; never give your opinion about anything, always use the Bible as your point of reference; never give your bank book, check book, or credit card to anyone; never co-sign for anybody but your husband/wife (debatable- smile). A wise man's heart guides his mouth, and his lips promote instruction (Proverbs 11:23 LAB). The fruit of the righteous is a tree of life, and he who wins souls is wise (Proverbs 11:30 LAB). Therefore Jesus said, "I am sending you out like sheep among wolves. Therefore, be as shrewd (wise) as snakes and as innocent as doves (Matthews 10:16 LAB). Blessed are the peacemakers, for they will be called sons/daughters of God (Matthews 5:9 LAB).

CHAPTER 20
<u>I'M STUCK LIKE GLUE</u>

Who shall separate me from the love of Christ: tribulation, distress, persecution, famine, nakedness, peril, or sword? I am persuaded, that neither death, life, angels, principalities, powers, things present, things to come, heights, depths, or any other creatures shall be able to separate me from the love of God, which is in Christ Jesus my Lord (Romans 8:35, 38-39).

I am now sixty-two years old. I have just retired from my job after twenty years of service. I am so blessed to see this time and season in my life. Many times I thought that I was not going to make it. I gave up on myself many times, but I never gave up on God. I have made many mistakes, and have even sinned since I have been save. But I have learned that, if you fall, don't lay there; get up, repent, and go forward. Don't make excuses. Admit you have done wrong, and ask God to forgive you. If we confess our sins, He is faithful and just, and will forgive us our sins, and purify us from all unrighteousness (1st John 1:9, LAB).

I love God more than ever before. I have been save for 43 years, and all through those years I have been learning how to live save. The longer I live, the more I learn about Him, for His yoke is easy and His burden is light. The more I learn to lean on Him, the easier my burdens become. Cast all your anxieties (cares) on Him because He cares for you. For we do not have a high priest who is unable to sympathize with our weakness, but we have one who has been tempted in every way, just as we have been; yet He was without sin. Let us then approach the throne of grace with confidence, so that we may receive mercy and find grace to help us in our time of need (Hebrews 4:15-16, LAB).

All I can say is, "To God be the glory for the things He has done with my life." There is a song that comes to mind that I used to sing years ago, "If anyone should ever write my life's story; you would be there between each line of pain and glory. Because Jesus, you are the best thing that ever happened to me." Since I have been save, I have said things, did things, and acted in ways that was not pleasing in God's sight. But, I never said that I don't want to be save anymore, and the thought never entered my mind. God has been, and yet is too good to me for me to give up on Him.

I have suffered many things: some because of my own during and some because God said to go through them. They were for my making and my breaking. For God, sometimes, has to break us before He can make us like the potter with the clay. God loves us enough to change us to what He has purposed and ordained for our lives to be. God really knows what is best for us in our lives: our marriages, our jobs, our families, and our friends. Trust in the Lord with all your heart, and lean not to your own understanding. In all your ways acknowledge Him, and He will make your paths straight (Proverbs 3:5-6, LAB). Again, I say, "To God be the glory for the things He has done with my life."

There are so many more things about my life that God has taken me through during the years that I have been saved. However, time will not allow me to write at this time about them all: Tonia and her arm, Craig and his legs, my grandson's sickness, my job, my second marriage, and Billy's death. Maybe one day, God will set me down, and I will take pen and pencil in hand and write again. For God is good, His mercies are new every morning, every day, every month, and every year. For year, after year, after year, God's Mercies are new!!!

ABOUT THE AUTHOR

Evangelist Lula Holliday accepted Christ as her Lord and Savior in 1962. She was licensed as an Evangelist Missionary of the Church of God in Christ in 1969 under the Pastorate of Elder Damon Wiggins. She has been a member of The Mount Sinai Cathedral C.O.G.I.C. in Brooklyn, New York for 34 years.

Evangelist Holliday worked with the Sunday School Department of the First Ecclesiastical Jurisdiction of Eastern New York under Sunday School Superintendent David Hall. She served as Executive Sunday School Superintendent for her church (Mt. Sinai Cathedral Church of God in Christ) for 20 years. She served as State Sunday School Superintendent for 10 years under Bishop CL Sexton and Bishop A. Baker. She served as the National Prayer Warrior for the Second Ecclesiastical Jurisdiction of Eastern New York. She also served with the State Women's Department Devotional Committee and Workshop Committee under the leadership of Supervisor Marion Vickers and Supervisor Louidell Green. She presently serves as the Outreach and Workshop Committee Coordinator of the Women's Department of the Bishop CL Sexton Memorial District.

Evangelist Holliday attended United Christian College and Bethel Bible School and received numerous certifications in Bible Studies. She is available for speaking engagements and workshops. She can be contacted my mail at 172-32 133rd Ave. #9G Jamaica, New York 11434; by phone at 718 712-7407; and by Email at heknewme2@peoplepc.com.

CPSIA information can be obtained at www.ICGtesting.com
265296BV00002B/2/A